Sainte-Marie Among the Hurons
The Jesuit Mission to the Huron Indians
1634 - 1649

SAINTE~MARIE

AMONG THE HURONS

a play by James W. Nichol

Talonbooks . Vancouver . Los Angeles . 1980

published with assistance from the Canada Council

Talonbooks   Talonbooks
201 1019 East Corodova   P.O. Box 42720
Vancouver   Los Angeles
British Columbia V6A 1M8   California 90042
Canada   U.S.A.

This book was typeset by Linda Gilbert, designed by
David Robinson and printed by Webcom for Talonbooks.

First printing: April 1980

Talonplays are edited by Peter Hay.

Sainte-Marie Among the Hurons was first published by
Playwrights Co-op, Toronto, Ontario.

Rights to produce *Sainte-Marie Among the Hurons*, in whole
or in part, in any medium by any group, amateur or
professional, are retained by the author and interested
persons are requested to apply to him at 15 Willowbank
Boulevard, Toronto, Ontario M4R 1B7.

Canadian Cataloguing in Publication Data

Nichol, James W., 1940—
       Sainte-Marie among the Hurons

       ISBN 0-88922-147-2 pa.

       1. Fort Ste. Marie, Ont. — Drama. 2. Jesuits —
Missions — Ontario — Drama. 3. Huron Indians —
Missions — Drama. I. Title.
PS8577.I29S3 1980   C812'.54   C80-901171-7
PR9199.3.N52S3 1980

Father Jean de Brébeuf — *"He who thinks of coming here for any other than God will have made a sad mistake. It is He alone and His cross that should be sought in running after these people, for if you strive for anything else, you will find nought but bodily and spiritual affliction."*

The Jesuit Relations, *1635*

Father Le Mercier — *"The Indians are quick to see how our doctrine conforms to reason, and how inhuman and senseless are their own superstitions."*

The Jesuit Relations, *1638*

Father Jerome Lalemont — *"It has happened very often, and has been remarked more than a hundred times, that in those places where we were most welcome, where we baptized most people, there it was, in fact, where they died most. On the contrary, in the cabins to which we were denied entrance, although they were sick to extremity, at the end of a few days one saw every person prosperously cured. We shall find in Heaven the secret but ever adorable judgments of God therein."*

The Jesuit Relations, *1641*

Father Jean de Brébeuf — *"I feel in me a great desire to die, in order to enjoy God. I feel a great aversion for all created things, which it will be necessary for me to leave at death. It is in God alone that my heart rests, and outside of Him, all is naught to me except for Him."*

The Jesuit Relations, *1635*

Sainte-Marie Among the Hurons was first performed at Theatre London in London, Ontario on November 19, 1974, with the following cast:

Blackrobe	Colin Fox
Martyr	John Goodlin
Broken Rock	August Schellenberg
Sleeping Water	Wayne Burnett
Ataenstic	Kip Longstaff
Iouskeha	Duncan Regehr
Shaman	Jim Schaefer
Young Woman	Irene Balser
Father Superior	Vincent Cole
Jesuits	Robert Vigod, Elias Zarou, Peter Orange, Peter Colley
Iroquois Prisoner	Jim Schaefer
Young Huron Man	Steve Hilton
Huron Men	Dale Flannigan, Gordon Garrett, Steve Hilton, Stuart Hughes, Eric Kennleyside, David Martin, Don Martin, Ken Scadden, Jim Schaefer, Michael Wyatt, Peter Colley, Peter Orange, Robert Vigod, Elias Zarou
Huron Women	Kim Ange, Irene Balser, Lori Broad, Phyllis Caissey, Sylvie Farrell, Janis Gott, Diana Jarvel, Colleen Kernohan, Noni McLean, Helen Slaght, Heather Vogan, Sonya Zierhofer
Huron Youths and Children	David Bigelow, Albert Brule, Karen Eck, Jamie Eck, David Hughes, Pam Oglesby

Directed by Heinar Piller
Set Design by Antonin Dimitrov
Lighting Design by David Wallett
Costume Design by Olga Dimitrov
Sound Score Composed and Directed by Berthold Carriere

Sainte-Marie Among the Hurons was also performed at the National Arts Centre in Ottawa, Ontario on January 10, 1977, with the following cast:

Blackrobe	Colin Fox
Martyr	Laurence Aubrey
Broken Rock	Jan Muszynski
Sleeping Water	Wayne Burnett
Father Superior	Hugh Webster
Father Henri	Richard McMillan
Father Daniel	Wilfred Dubé
Iroquois Warriors	Ron MacKenzie, David Marion, Gregory Ellwand, Ben Freedman

Directed by Heinar Piller
Set and Costume Design by Art Penson
Lighting Design by David Wallett
Sound by Allan Rae

LIST OF CHARACTERS

BLACKROBE, *a Jesuit priest.*
MARTYR, *Blackrobe's conscience.*
BROKEN ROCK, *a Huron Indian.*
SLEEPING WATER, *a Huron Indian.*
FATHER SUPERIOR
FATHER HENRI } *Jesuit priests.*
FATHER DANIEL
FOUR IROQUOIS WARRIORS.

PLACE

Huronia.

TIME

1634-1649.

SET

Upstage, a scrim is hung, which is used for various sky effects. Downstage, a little from the scrim, is a series of tall pine poles, sharpened somewhat at the ends, extending irregularly across the stage to represent Huron palisades and the forests of Huronia. High ramps are set up on the palisades, exiting left and right, somewhat obscured by more pine poles set in front of them. The ramps join at centrestage at the top of an earthen ramp that slants downstage to level stage centre. The top of the ramp can also be reached from extreme upstage, directly behind, out of view of the audience. There are various exits between pine poles left and right of the earthen ramp at stage level, below the palisade ramps. The bare forestage has easy access to the left and right audience aisles. At extreme downstage centre, projected into the audience a little, and a few feet above the main stage level, is a tiny stage area. This area will be used most often by the MARTYR, but will also be used by BLACKROBE and once by FATHER SUPERIOR. From this area, the main stage level can be reached by steps or by a short leap. It contains a pit that the MARTYR uses several times for entrances and exits. The general effect should be that the stage is about to be overwhelmed by the tall brooding pine poles that overhang it, making the downstage area a focus of energy and stress, a kind of bear pit or crucible.

ACT ONE
Scene One

*The stage is in darkness. After a moment, BLACKROBE
enters, moves to downstage centre and lights a candle.
Slowly, a soft light falls on him, the rest of the stage
remaining in darkness. BLACKROBE is kneeling, staring
at the flame of the candle. He wears his long black cassock
and wide-brimmed hat, a white rope belt and a crucifix.*

MARTYR: *from the darkness, crouched downstage on
    the elevated stage area*   Don't be afraid.

BLACKROBE: *not turning towards the voice, not
    alarmed, seemingly deep in thought*   I am not afraid.

MARTYR: Don't tremble.

BLACKROBE: I don't tremble.

*The lights come up on the MARTYR, who is dressed in
filthy rags. One side of his face has been horribly disfigured
and his long hair fans out in disarray about his head. He
gives the impression of having catlike quickness and
indomitable spirit.*

MARTYR: *standing up slowly* They dressed me in a cloak stiff with wax. They tied me to an axletree.

BLACKROBE: *not looking at him* Yes!

MARTYR: I burned like a candle. In Nero's garden.

The MARTYR leaps lightly to the main stage and approaches BLACKROBE stealthily. BLACKROBE does not look at him, but stares intensely at something in mid-air.

MARTYR: Precious Réjean, the mysterious child who was always reading his Book of Martyrs. Oh, such a long time ago! I stepped out of the pages and into your mind. And don't you remember how every night your mother knelt beside you and prayed for your soul?

BLACKROBE: I remember the house, in sunlight. The rolling hills. The laneway to the town.

MARTYR: *crouching closer to him* And when you closed your eyes, I came to you, all aflame!

BLACKROBE: The airy kitchen, the long straight stairs, my room with my books and the little window and . . .

MARTYR: *at his ear* Jesus, hanging crucified on the wall. You wish you were back in France, don't you? Tucked in your bed. I think you are afraid!

BLACKROBE: No! *He stands up abruptly.* I begged for this mission. You saw me there!

MARTYR: Yes, I saw you! *He laughs and moves away from BLACKROBE.* And I saw him too. Father Robillaird! Pink and fat! Sitting in his grand room, seated on his grand . . . chair. *He sits on the edge of the elevated area.* "Dear Réjean," he said, "I fear your constitution is not strong enough to stand up to the rigours of the new world."

BLACKROBE: *turning to the MARTYR and speaking as if to FATHER ROBILLAIRD* Christ will sustain me.

MARTYR: But the savages, Father! I fear your nerves would not stand the strain. Why, it has not been two weeks . . .

BLACKROBE: I know now what Christ would command from this poor servant. My days and nights have been filled with praying.

MARTYR: Not two weeks, may I remind you, since you returned to us from your rest at home. Your unfortunate illness . . .

BLACKROBE: I am not a teacher of rich men's sons!

MARTYR: To break down and cry in the middle of a class on Pliny, the Younger. Extraordinary!

BLACKROBE: Please! I know now what I have been called to do!

MARTYR: A divine revelation?

BLACKROBE: I will not fail!

MARTYR: This time? *He dismisses him.* Oh, alright. . . . We will consider and let you know.

He lies down, his back to BLACKROBE, resting his head on his hands.

BLACKROBE: When?

MARTYR: Father! In due course.

BLACKROBE: *advancing on the MARTYR, who continues to look the other way* In three years! And was I a penitent? Was I a beggar? Why did you keep me in your anterooms, send me little notes of regret, delay meetings, defer decisions? To test me, wasn't it? To dissect me! To draw out my nerves! But I endured it all, remained steadfast, and so, at last, I had to be recognized. I would not go away from your door! I forced him to deal with this pest! With me!

MARTYR: *shouting out joyfully, his arms spread wide* Father Robillaird is five thousand miles away! Praise the Lord! Why do you get so excited about those three years? We have been waiting for this moment for thirty years! Ever since you found me in your Golden Book of Martyrs. Splendid child! All those other brats played at soldiers and sailors, but not you, Réjean. You played at dying. *He is teetering on the edge of the elevated stage, mocking BLACKROBE.* Crucified on the high clean edge of death . . . painless, like falling asleep.

He falls lightly onto the main stage, then curls up, as if he were asleep.

BLACKROBE: It was not a childish thing! I was . . . serious!

MARTYR: *still mockingly* Even sleeping, your Book of Martyrs shone in the dark beside your bed. Even dreaming, I hung on an axletree and burned in your mind. *He creeps towards BLACKROBE.* But I did not play with my life, Réjean. And there was a reason for my death! Don't you know that I was called to testify for Christ?

BLACKROBE: Not only you! I swear on my soul that I understand everything. I am called!

MARTYR: Oh, that's good, Réjean. Very good! For we are all alone in this wilderness. The savages surround us. Now we must be about our work!

He leaps up onto the elevated stage.

BLACKROBE: Wait! Don't leave!

14

MARTYR: I have burned for you through the years,
never once letting you forget it is Christ we seek beyond
these flames. Shall I forsake you now, when we are so
close to finding Him?   *He speaks in a whisper.*
All else in this world is darkness.

*The MARTYR exits slowly into the pit and disappears.
BLACKROBE stares after him for a moment, then kneels
and prays.*

BLACKROBE: '   My Lord, you know that I have come
to this land as an apostle. "Other sheep have I," You
said. "Those must I also bring." Oh, Jesus, bless my
apostleship! It has begun!

Scene Two

*The sky begins to lighten with early morning colours. The
tops of the dark pine poles become visible against the sky.
The dark silhouette of BROKEN ROCK stands against the
sky at the top of the earthen ramp. BLACKROBE, sensing
someone behind him, turns slowly to look up towards
BROKEN ROCK. The lights come up slowly.*

*BROKEN ROCK wears a loose-fitting deerskin garment,
draped over one shoulder with a tear for the arm to go
through, and then, under the other arm, tied to the waist
with rawhide, falling to his knees and split on both sides
to allow freedom of leg movement. This garment, the only
clothing he wears, combines a savage and a senatorial
impression. His arms are marked with a dull red ochre pattern
of straight and curved lines and circles. A thick black line
of face paint, outlined in yellow, curves under both eyes
and over the bridge of the nose. His hair is long and braided,
the two braids lying against his chest. He is barefoot.*

*BROKEN ROCK stares down coldly at BLACKROBE,
and then begins to advance slowly towards him, down the*

ramp. BLACKROBE stands up, frightened, then backs up a little, trying to look relaxed and friendly. BROKEN ROCK circles around him slowly, silently, then takes the candle from BLACKROBE and slowly squeezes out the flame. Suddenly, with a blood-chilling scream, he breaks the candle and feints a move towards BLACKROBE, who flinches and jumps back towards the palisades, stage right. Immediately, SLEEPING WATER leaps from the palisade ramp above and with a whoop lands beside BLACKROBE. BLACKROBE is surprised and frightened and runs back a little towards BROKEN ROCK.

BROKEN ROCK: *laughing loudly* Ha! Ha! Ha! He jumps about like a rabbit!

SLEEPING WATER is barefoot and wears only a loincloth of deerskin. He has no face or body paint, but he has amulets of bone and stone hanging about his neck. His countenance does not have the fierce strength of BROKEN ROCK, but there is nobility and sensitivity to his features.

SLEEPING WATER: Look at him shiver! Even his nose quivers!

BLACKROBE: *smiling and looking a little relieved* Sleeping Water!

SLEEPING WATER: *ignoring him and walking downstage* Something must be making him nervous.

BROKEN ROCK: *indicating the audience* Our people make him nervous.

BLACKROBE: No. I'm perfectly happy!

SLEEPING WATER: Perhaps he's just eager to hop about after such a long journey.

BROKEN ROCK: Perhaps he's deciding which way to run.

BLACKROBE: No!

SLEEPING WATER: *going up the right aisle a little
and addressing the audience*   This rabbit's name . . .
is Réjean.

BLACKROBE takes off his hat.

BROKEN ROCK: *addressing the audience, overriding
SLEEPING WATER*   This thing . . . is what the French
demanded we bring back with us. It is not enough that
we trade our priceless fur to them for their useless bits
of metal. . . .   *He smiles slyly.*   Now we must
entertain their half-wits! He is nothing to us, but I
wonder why it was so important to the French that
he come into our land? I ask myself. . . . What is it
about this thing?

SLEEPING WATER: *laughing, coming back to level
stage centre*   What harm can there be in him?

BROKEN ROCK: *turning on SLEEPING WATER*
There can be harm in all things!

SLEEPING WATER: Look for yourself. He is gentle as
a rabbit, as you said.   *He speaks again to the audience.*
He lit our fires on our journey back from Kebec. He
traded with the Algonkin for fish to feed us on our way.

BROKEN ROCK: I was not cold. I was not starving.
Haven't we made that same trip many times before?
I would rather he had tumbled out of your canoe and
drowned, than be standing here in our land. But for the
French, he would be swimming with the fishes now!
They said — take him with you or bring us no more
furs. We will not do business otherwise. I can see the
advantage works both ways. He is a hostage in our land,
and so I am prepared to tolerate him a little.   *He turns
to SLEEPING WATER.*   But don't expect me to treat
him like a man. This half thing! The French runners at
least are men. They attack our women like starving

wolves!   *He advances on BLACKROBE.*   We are not selfish. They go back to Kebec with their bellies full.

BROKEN ROCK laughs a little. BLACKROBE smiles uncertainly.

BROKEN ROCK: And you? Are you hungry?

BLACKROBE: No! I am not hungry.

BROKEN ROCK: Ah . . . the Raven speaks! It would be best for you to remain silent. Try not to move. Be like a stone. Otherwise you may offend the gods.   *He turns and runs lightly up the left aisle to midpoint, then turns back.*   If our harvest fails . . . if the fish do not run to our nets . . . I will speak in the councils for your death.

He exits up the aisle.

BLACKROBE retreats a little upstage left. He is visibly shaken. He sits down on the log supports of the earthen ramp, putting his hat down and forgetting SLEEPING WATER, who, looking amused, regards him for a moment.

SLEEPING WATER: Are you afraid to die?

BLACKROBE: No! I think it would be a great pleasure.

SLEEPING WATER: *going up to him*   Then why do you shake so much?

BLACKROBE: *getting up and moving downstage a little* The air is cold.

SLEEPING WATER: *laughing*   How could you feel cold under that blanket? Besides, the sun is out. It is hot.

BLACKROBE: Is it?   *He looks up at the sky.*   I must be cold inside.

SLEEPING WATER: When I first went to Kebec and saw the French ships with their great masts and sails . . . I was cold inside.   *He sits on the ramp.*   It's not unnatural.

BLACKROBE: *looking with interest at SLEEPING WATER*   No, I suppose not.   *He moves to him.* Sleeping Water, why is Broken Rock angry? I have not insulted him, have I?

SLEEPING WATER: He doesn't know whether he likes this French trade or not. He reaches out with his one hand, but his other hand is behind his back. The trade is too one-sided, he says. It makes him nervous.

BLACKROBE: *sitting down beside him*   But I have nothing to do with the trade. I have come because . . . *He catches himself.*   . . . because I want to learn about the Huron people. Surely he can see that I can do no possible harm. How could I? One man against thirty thousand!   *He laughs.*   How ridiculous! The man must be a fool!

SLEEPING WATER: *rising*   No! Broken Rock is not a fool.   *He moves downstage a little.*   He is a leader of our people. A hunter. A great warrior. His mother was also my mother. Since I was old enough to walk, he has shared everything with me. He is myself.

BLACKROBE: *getting up and moving to him*   I am not asking you to go against your brother! I have nothing but peace and love in my heart for him, and for you and all your people. But you are the only one who was kind to me on our long voyage into your country. I think of you as my friend! All I ask is for your help if Broken Rock should speak out against me. I have not even made a beginning here!

SLEEPING WATER: Beginning? To what?

BLACKROBE: *hesitating for a moment*   I . . . I'm not perfect in your language. I do not understand your

19

politics . . . or your history. I can't be sent back with
so little knowledge of the Huron. My people would be
disappointed.

SLEEPING WATER: Broken Rock has no great power.
All things are decided in council and he has but one
voice. He would die before he'd go against the council.
The signs remain good. The gods must be pleased that
you are here, so don't be so uneasy. You should stand
firm. Broken Rock does not like weakness.

BLACKROBE: *stung*   I am not weak!

SLEEPING WATER: *quietly reassuring him*   Neither
are we . . . friend!

Scene Three

*SLEEPING WATER moves up the ramp and disappears
upstage, over the ramp and behind the palisades. The lights
go down and the Huron Chorus and music come up,
coming from all around the theatre — drums and rattles and
a steady Hia hia hia hia hia hiaha! Hia hia hia hia hia hia
hiaha! The sky becomes a red glow as BLACKROBE moves
downstage into a spotlight. He is surrounded by sound,
and looks about apprehensively. The sound builds.*

BLACKROBE: *to the audience*   People . . . I would
tell you a story.   *He has to shout against the sound.*
I have come to you with a message of great hope! I am
the way to your salvation!   *He moves to extreme
downstage right.*   Please listen to me!   *The sound
continues.*   Listen!

*Immediately, all sound stops and the lights come up. There
is absolute silence. BLACKROBE looks around at the
audience, then moves up the right aisle a little. He is very
nervous and hesitant as he talks directly to the audience.*

BLACKROBE: People, listen to me. In the beginning,
   there was nothing of the sky and the earth, except a
   vast expanse of water. And there was no light, but an
   absolute darkness across the face of the water.

BROKEN ROCK appears high on the palisade, stage left,
watching BLACKROBE.

BLACKROBE: And God came forth and made light out
   of the darkness so that the water could be seen.

BROKEN ROCK laughs a little, a low sound which is
mirthless. BLACKROBE sees him, hesitates a second, then
continues.

BLACKROBE: And . . . God split the depth of the water
   in two parts . . .

BROKEN ROCK laughs louder, crossing to the top of the
earthen ramp. BLACKROBE tries to ignore him.

BLACKROBE: . . . And God placed the sky and all things
   of the sky between the two parts!

BROKEN ROCK laughs loud and long. BLACKROBE turns
to face him.

BROKEN ROCK: Listen to the half-wit!   *He turns to*
   the audience.   In the beginning, Ataenstic, the mother
   of all men, lived in a forest above the sky. One day she
   was out hunting and her dog ran a bear into a deep cave.
   Ataenstic followed and she fell into a hole in the
   darkness and she fell into the sky.   *He walks slowly*
   down the ramp.   Like a leaf in the wind, she fell
   and fell and plunged into a great sea of water below.
   Turtle rose up out of the sea carrying the earth and
   Ataenstic on his back. . . .   *He looks at BLACKROBE.*
   . . . And that was the beginning of the world!

SLEEPING WATER enters at stage level, upstage right
from under the palisade. He moves towards stage centre,

watching BLACKROBE, who comes down the aisle to the stage, crossing with his back to BROKEN ROCK.

BLACKROBE: *addressing the audience* God . . . Almighty God . . . took the clay of the earth and from this clay He made a man. He took a rib from the side of the man and from this rib He made a woman and they were the first man and the first woman on this earth!

BROKEN ROCK: Ataenstic gave birth to two sons. The older of the two was called Iouskeha. He struck down his brother with the antlers of a deer and this was the first murder that the earth knew. Iouskeha fled through the forest, afraid to face Ataenstic, for he had murdered her favoured son.

BLACKROBE: *going up the left aisle, ignoring BROKEN ROCK* God gave the first man and the first woman dominion over all the creatures of the earth, the fish of the water, the birds of the air, the animals of the woods.

BROKEN ROCK: Iouskeha took a pointed stick and he thrust the stick through the side of a frog and water poured out and rushed through the forests and made rivers and lakes. He took his bow and shot an arrow into the foot of each of the animals of the woods so that men would be able to catch them. Only the wolf escaped.

BLACKROBE: *coming back onstage towards BROKEN ROCK, now talking directly to him* God became angry with the first man and the first woman and he drove them away from the garden he had provided for them and he caused the woman and all women thereafter to bear children in great pain. And he caused the man and all men thereafter to toil mightily against the earth all the days of their lives!

BROKEN ROCK: *to BLACKROBE* Ataenstic cursed Iouskeha and she cursed all men who would follow him from the darkening ages down to this time! She is the moon and she causes death in all mankind and she is therefore evil!

BLACKROBE: God ... Almighty Lord of Heavenly Hosts!

BROKEN ROCK: Iouskeha is the sun! He provides all things for men and is therefore good!   *He advances on BLACKROBE.*   They were the beginning of our world. They are with us yet. They rule over the gods of water, stone and fire. The gods of lightning, thunder and wind. The gods are everywhere and everywhere must bow to Ataenstic and Iouskeha!

BROKEN ROCK and BLACKROBE stand very close together, staring at each other. BLACKROBE is amazed at BROKEN ROCK's doctrine, not knowing what else to say.

BLACKROBE: No!

SLEEPING WATER: *a warning, moving towards BLACK-ROBE and BROKEN ROCK*   Blackrobe!

BROKEN ROCK: *putting his hand up to silence SLEEPING WATER, still staring at BLACKROBE*   Raven ... are you deaf? Did you not hear what I just said?

BLACKROBE: There is only one world, Broken Rock, and only one God.

BROKEN ROCK: *quietly, but threateningly*   I have told you how Ataenstic fell from the sky. Do you not believe what I said? Am I a liar?

SLEEPING WATER: *coming between BROKEN ROCK and BLACKROBE, trying to make it a joke*   Broken Rock, the Blackrobe's confused. He thinks he is still in his own world. We must be a people in a dream to him.   *He laughs.*   He does not know he is awake!

BROKEN ROCK: Then tell him it is a dream . . . and the portent of his dream is one of danger. I will not waste my breath on such a fool!

BROKEN ROCK turns abruptly, walks up the earthen ramp, and disappears upstage. SLEEPING WATER and BLACK-ROBE look at each other for a moment.

SLEEPING WATER: You are a fool! You don't know what world you're in!

SLEEPING WATER turns and disappears below the palisade, stage left. The lights go down, as BLACKROBE turns from watching SLEEPING WATER disappear, and walks down-stage. There is only one spotlight on BLACKROBE; the rest of the stage is in darkness.

BLACKROBE: *lost in his own fantasy*   "But I, being full of the Holy Ghost, looked up steadfastly into heaven and saw the glory of God and Jesus standing on the right hand of God. And I said, behold, I see the heavens opened, and the Son of Man standing on the right hand of God. Then they cried out with a loud voice, and stopped their ears, and ran upon me with one accord . . . and stoned me. I cried with a loud voice, Lord, lay not this sin to their charge. And when I said this, I fell asleep."

The lights come up on the MARTYR, who is coming out of the pit.

MARTYR: And there was blood coming from St. Stephen's mouth. And blood on his face.

BLACKROBE: *not turning to him*   Did you hear them? They won't listen to me. They call me a fool.

MARTYR: Are you happy? Do you think you are suffering?

BLACKROBE: *angrily*   No, I am not suffering! I am not anything!

24

*The MARTYR comes off the elevated stage area and walks
a little upstage of BLACKROBE. He speaks mockingly.*

MARTYR: The would-be apostle of Christ! Réjean, fisher
of men! It has always been easier to love Christ in secret
than to be His witness to the world. Just play at it,
Réjean. No one will know the difference here. Forget
Christ crucified.

BLACKROBE: My love for Christ consumes me. But it
does not make me strong. How much easier it was to
say His Name at home to the rows and rows of freshly
scrubbed faces in front of me. "Lord Jesus, Our
Saviour," I said!

MARTYR: Until the day you could say it no more,
weeping at your desk. So many tears! The children
were frightened.

BLACKROBE: My dear Lord, I wept for you!

MARTYR: But it is not good enough. Did Jesus Himself
not sweat blood before He took one step towards the
Cross? Did I not burn? Tears are nothing!

BLACKROBE: I am not afraid to die! I long for it!
Everything on this earth is wretched to me!

MARTYR: *laughing at him*   Everybody dies, Réjean!
But who dies for Christ? Who shall have Paradise? Who
shall free these people from the dark and lead them to
the everlasting light?   *He advances on him.*   Not
you! You will play at suffering! You will weep a river!

BLACKROBE slowly sinks to his knees.

MARTYR: You will condemn their souls to hell! And
your own! You would be a victim? You, who won't
take the first step towards the Cross? And Jesus, nailed
there like a piece of raw meat?

BLACKROBE: Oh, but I will!

MARTYR: *quietly, after a pause*   Then there you are,
Réjean. . . .   *He indicates the audience, steps back,
then begins to move upstage.*   . . . They are waiting
for you. Do not betray us.

He disappears stage left, beneath the palisade.

*BLACKROBE stays kneeling for a moment, downstage.
He takes off the crucifix from around his neck, holds it for
a moment before him, and then, with determination, he
gets to his feet and steps up onto the elevated stage. He
stares at the audience and holds the crucifix in front of
him for them to see.*

BLACKROBE: A long time ago, a man was put to death
on a wooden cross, such as this. The man was the Son of
the one and only God. I bring you a revelation of this
one true God . . .

*The lights come up on BROKEN ROCK as he enters stage
right and slowly crosses to the ramp, dragging a corpse
wrapped in beaver pelts on a litter made up of two long
poles. He drags it up the ramp a little way and then gently
lets it down. BLACKROBE sees BROKEN ROCK, then
turns back to the audience, trying to keep their attention
away from BROKEN ROCK.*

BLACKROBE: . . . And His Son, Jesus Christ. Listen to
me and believe, for the sake of your eternal souls! When
Mary, the mother of Jesus, was but a young girl . . .

*SLEEPING WATER enters from under the palisade, stage
left, carrying a large clay pot and stone scrapers. He puts
the pot down beside the corpse, then he and BROKEN
ROCK carefully unwrap the pelts. BLACKROBE glances
back at them and then continues.*

BLACKROBE: . . . She had a vision of an Angel, and the Angel said to her, "Mary, blessed art thou among women, for you have found favour with God and you shall conceive in thy womb . . . and bring forth a son . . ."

The beaver pelts are removed. The corpse is propped up so that the audience can see that it is the partially decomposed corpse of an old woman with long grey hair.

BLACKROBE: . . . "And you shall call him . . ."

Reacting to the audience, he turns to look upstage at SLEEPING WATER and BROKEN ROCK. He sees the corpse and is horrified.

BLACKROBE: . . . "Jesus!"

BLACKROBE steps down off the elevated stage level and slowly moves upstage towards SLEEPING WATER. BROKEN ROCK moves up the earthen ramp, almost to the top, and sits down, his legs crossed, his arms hanging loosely at his sides, his head down, staring at the ground. SLEEPING WATER starts to peel back the scalp from the skull of the corpse, throwing pieces into the clay pot.

BLACKROBE: *fascinated and horrified*   What are you doing?

SLEEPING WATER: *looking up, but continuing to work carefully*   She died at the end of the winter. The snow was beginning to melt.

BLACKROBE: Who is she?

SLEEPING WATER: We placed her on a platform high above our heads so that she would be close to the sky.

BLACKROBE: *urgently*   Who is she?

SLEEPING WATER: *looking up at him*   She is my mother.

BLACKROBE covers his mouth and steps back, feeling ill.

SLEEPING WATER: She is Broken Rock's mother.
    He continues to work.   I am preparing her for the
    feast of the dead.

*The sound of the Huron Chorus comes up, very low and
slow, chanting a lament.*

SLEEPING WATER: The bones of all the dead of our
    nation will be scraped clean and prepared for the feast.
    I tell you, Blackrobe, the air will be heavy with the smell
    of burning flesh. The night sky will glow from the clan
    of the Bear to the Deer, from the clan of the Cord to
    the Rock.

*BROKEN ROCK joins the lament, which is a wailing sound,
softly at first and then louder, still staring at the ground,
his body seemingly lifeless. His voice rises and falls.*

SLEEPING WATER: It has happened so, twice before
    in my lifetime and many times before that, back to the
    creation of the world. We will march to the pit.

BLACKROBE: What pit? What do you mean?

SLEEPING WATER: A great hole in the earth where the
    bones of all our dead are tumbled together. From there,
    the souls of the dead depart with Iouskeha across the
    sky to the other side of the night. They live with him
    there for all the rest of time, on the very edge of the
    world.   *He looks up at BLACKROBE.*   But this
    world is different from your world. Our gods are
    different from yours.

BLACKROBE: *backing up a little*   Oh yes, I know who
    your god is now! Iouskeha . . . prince of darkness!
    He kneels, staring at the corpse.   Oh my Lord, I am
    at the very gates of hell!

BROKEN ROCK and SLEEPING WATER look at BLACK-ROBE, neither one of them moving. There is complete silence. BLACKROBE continues to stare at the corpse.

The lights go down and out.

Scene Four

The sound of a winter wind comes up. Slowly, the lights come up to half, on a bleak winter evening just before dark. The stage is empty. After a moment, BLACKROBE enters from under the palisade, stage right, his feet wrapped in scraps of cloth. He pulls a torn grey blanket more tightly about his shoulders to protect him from the cold. He looks tired as he starts out doggedly to shuffle through the snow, crossing towards downstage left. SLEEPING WATER, wrapped in a fur robe and fur leggings, appears at the top of the earthen ramp. He sees BLACKROBE crossing below him and watches him for a second.

SLEEPING WATER: Blackrobe! There's a storm coming. It will be here soon. Come in by the fire and keep warm.

BLACKROBE: *turning back to him*   No. I promised to go to the village on the river.

SLEEPING WATER: *coming down the ramp to level stage centre, teasing him*   Who did you promise? Yourself? *He laughs.*   What a strange man you are! Don't you ever get tired of talking about your God? I see you walking from village to village and everywhere they laugh at you. Broken Rock says you enjoy the laughter.

BLACKROBE: *coming back to him*   I do! It warms me . . . like a fire!

SLEEPING WATER: Then stand by the laughter to keep warm. It makes no difference to me.

They look at each other for a moment, then BLACKROBE turns and walks towards stage left.

SLEEPING WATER: Wait. I'll give you a robe of beaver skins.

BLACKROBE: I don't want it!

He continues to walk away.

SLEEPING WATER: I have seen trees split in the cold. That thing you wear is useless.

BLACKROBE turns back to him.

SLEEPING WATER: The wolf will be dancing on the snow tonight . . . just to keep his feet warm.

BLACKROBE: *coming back to him, laughing*   Sleeping Water! Good and kind soul! When it seems I am only a shadow and no one can see me, I think of you! You see me. You hear me.

SLEEPING WATER: And why not?   *He laughs.* What have I to fear?

BLACKROBE: Broken Rock?

SLEEPING WATER: Why do you say that? I am separate from Broken Rock!

BLACKROBE: And yet it seems to me he desires it the other way. You must agree with everything he says. You must do everything he does.   *He turns away from SLEEPING WATER and moves downstage.* Oh, this land, cut off from God. It is an unholy place. I think of Iouskeha . . . and I think of Satan. I think of this place on the other side of the night . . . and I think of hell.

SLEEPING WATER: Do you say that I'm not a man?
Do you say I'm still following Broken Rock about like
a boy?

BLACKROBE: I know that you and Broken Rock
delivered up your mother to Iouskeha. I did see that.
Remembering.   When my mother died, the heavens wept!
She was so good! So gentle! I was . . . shattered. I wept,
as I always do. But even so, I knew my mother was with
Jesus, glorified in heaven, shining triumphant and radiant
above her life. Above this . . . wretched world . . . that
would have her die in filth trying to bring forth one
more child into this desolation! Oh, she had loved Jesus
with a love so vast and pure! Even in my tears, even in
anguish, I was comforted by the glory that I knew held her
all around. Shining! I picked up my wounded life and
gave it to Jesus, who took my mother to Him, who loved
her as I loved her!   *He turns to SLEEPING WATER.*
But Broken Rock . . . and you . . .

SLEEPING WATER: What?

BLACKROBE: Your mother . . .

SLEEPING WATER: What of her?

BLACKROBE: Oh, Sleeping Water, you gave her soul to
Iouskeha to drag down to the torture posts of hell!

SLEEPING WATER: You don't understand. My mother
has journeyed to our honoured dead. She walks in great
joy again.

BLACKROBE: It's you who don't understand! Before
the creation of the world, there was a god, your god,
Iouskeha. In pride and envy, he rose up against Almighty
God, and he was hurled from heaven and he fell into a
pit of everlasting darkness and fire. But Iouskeha cannot
die. He can only suffer. And now, in his suffering, he
curses Almighty God and he crawls out along the edge of
the world. In trickery and disguise, in sun and moon, he

steals the souls of the dead from God. Your mother's soul, he stole from God!

SLEEPING WATER: He has taken my mother's soul . . .

BLACKROBE: To hell! To fire and torture! To everlasting anguish!

SLEEPING WATER: My mother lives in a village on the other side of the night. Iouskeha . . .

BLACKROBE: Is Satan! The whole world knows this but you. Your people are his slaves, trapped in this wilderness. That is why the world has sent me. To tell you this. To save you, Sleeping Water. Your soul.

SLEEPING WATER: My soul is not in danger.

BLACKROBE: Oh, but it is! You are just too blind to see!   *He touches SLEEPING WATER's amulets.* Do you really think you'll be saved by the little demons that live in these things? Or by Broken Rock?

SLEEPING WATER: *pushing him away*   Stay away! You have said enough!

BLACKROBE: Why have I said enough? I am here only because of you! When I gave my mother's soul to God, she rose up to heaven in light and glory. When you stripped your mother's flesh off as if she were an animal, you condemned her soul to hell!

SLEEPING WATER: No!

BLACKROBE: That is the truth of the world, Sleeping Water. Only through Jesus can your soul be saved. Only by coming to me!

SLEEPING WATER: Liar!

SLEEPING WATER turns and quickly exits under the palisades, stage left. BLACKROBE watches after him for a moment.

BLACKROBE: Oh yes, in time, the savages will become like angels. Oh yes! They'll lift their voices like a celestial chorus. To God!

Scene Five

The lights go down and out. The sound of the wind comes up. The lights come up a cold winter blue.

BROKEN ROCK, in a great state of excitement, enters over the ramp upstage and comes down to level stage centre, followed by SLEEPING WATER. They both wear heavy fur robes and fur leggings.

BROKEN ROCK: Ha! Ha! What a chase! Did you see how I ran?

SLEEPING WATER: *less enthusiastic*   Like a great spirit, Broken Rock.

BROKEN ROCK: Did you see how I seized him?

SLEEPING WATER: Like death, Broken Rock.

BROKEN ROCK: "Sing your warrior's song," I said. "Sing it now!" And all he could do was crawl about on his hands and knees and spit blood in the snow! "Iroquois dog! Sing a death chant. Old man! Weasel spy!"   *He looks at SLEEPING WATER.*   Did you hear me? "I'll look after you well, my friend," I said. "All this winter. And in the spring, I'll cook your flesh before your eyes!"

Laughing, he puts his arms around SLEEPING WATER.
BLACKROBE enters at the top of the stage right aisle. He
wanders slowly down to the stage, wrapped in a ragged grey
blanket, his feet wrapped in rags, mumbling his "Hail Mary's"
to himself.

BROKEN ROCK: The Raven. Cackling to itself.
    Half-mad. Come in, Sleeping Water. Let it die on its
    own.

He turns and exits briskly under the palisade, stage right,
as the lights start to go down.

BLACKROBE: *to himself, not seeing SLEEPING WATER*
    Hail Mary, full of grace; the Lord is with thee; blessed
    art thou amongst women, and blessed is the fruit of
    thy womb, Jesus. Holy Mary, Mother of God, pray for
    us sinners now and at the hour of our death. Amen.

BLACKROBE crosses himself, then pulls the blanket tighter
around him as the wind comes up. The lights are very low,
denoting a winter's night. He crosses downstage left and,
as he walks, he hunches up, bracing himself against the cold
wind, moving his feet heavily through the snow. SLEEPING
WATER, upstage, follows him across to the left without
BLACKROBE realizing he's there. He watches from the
shadows as BLACKROBE stands still for a moment, then
quickly unwraps his blanket and lays it out on the snow.
He kneels on it and unhooks his cassock, letting it fall down
about his waist, leaving him naked from the waist up against
the cold which rocks him back, like a blow.

BLACKROBE: *spreading his arms wide*   See what I
    do, mother? For you, mother . . . your son . . . a holy
    man. . . . Oh, mother, let me come home!

He closes his eyes and his body begins to shake with cold,
but he continues to hold his arms open. He begins to groan
softly. SLEEPING WATER takes off his fur robe, rushes
to BLACKROBE and throws it over his shoulders.

SLEEPING WATER: Would you kill yourself?

BLACKROBE holds the fur robe tightly about himself and bends over, his face almost touching the ground.

SLEEPING WATER: I told you. The cold cracks the trees. It will turn your blood to stone!

BLACKROBE: The Son of God was nailed to a cross. They wrapped a crown of thorns about His poor head. They crucified Him!

SLEEPING WATER: We can't stay in this spot much longer. We must go back.

BLACKROBE struggles to his feet. The robe falls from his shoulders as he pulls on his cassock.

SLEEPING WATER: It is dangerous to wander at night so far from the village. Your tracks could be lost in the snow.   *He watches BLACKROBE for a moment.* Why do you do this thing, hidden from our sight?

BLACKROBE: Christ suffered for me. That is why I suffer for Him.

SLEEPING WATER: He must be a very fierce god to make you do such a thing.   *He pulls on his heavy robe again.*   I will give you the beaver skin robe. That blanket is not enough.

BLACKROBE: It is too much. I would walk through the snow naked as a child, but I must not allow myself such freedom. I must hold steady! There is a difference between suffering for Christ at the hands of others and afflicting oneself with pain. I must be careful! I must be strong in my devotion!

SLEEPING WATER: You are strong. This God of yours makes you strong. Broken Rock would be surprised.

To kneel in the snow and let your blood freeze! He
could not do that. It takes great strength.

BLACKROBE: It takes great love, Sleeping Water.

SLEEPING WATER moves towards the left, away from
BLACKROBE. The sound of the wind dies down.

SLEEPING WATER: This God of yours? He is powerful?

BLACKROBE: He is very powerful!

SLEEPING WATER: Have you seen Him?

BLACKROBE: *following SLEEPING WATER*   In my
mind. In my dreams. Throughout the length and breadth
of my body, I know Him!

SLEEPING WATER: *abruptly turning away*   We talk
too much! The fires of the longhouse are better than this
bitter cold!

He moves upstage left, retracing his steps, and crosses to
centrestage.

BLACKROBE: Why do you ask me such questions?
He follows SLEEPING WATER.   Would you ask me
more? Oh, my friend, anything! I will tell you whatever
you would know!

SLEEPING WATER: I wish to know nothing!   *There is*
a pause, then he turns to BLACKROBE.   This God
of yours . . . he is stronger than Iouskeha?

BLACKROBE: My God is the Almighty God. I have told
you, He banished Iouskeha to the outer darkness for
all time!

SLEEPING WATER: What you said about the feast of
the dead, about my mother's soul; you have confused me!
My soul cries out!

BLACKROBE: *taking a step towards SLEEPING WATER*
Yes?

*BROKEN ROCK appears up on the palisade stage left,
above BLACKROBE. BLACKROBE does not see him, but
SLEEPING WATER does.*

BLACKROBE: What is it? Say it then! *He rushes up
to SLEEPING WATER and takes him by the arms.*
Say it!

SLEEPING WATER: *pushing BLACKROBE violently
away* Nothing! Get away! *He tries to compose
himself.* Go in. You are cold, go in by the fire.

BLACKROBE: But you must come in too!

SLEEPING WATER: *harshly* Go in!

*BLACKROBE looks at him, mystified, and then turns and
disappears through one of the openings under the palisade,
stage left. SLEEPING WATER looks at BROKEN ROCK,
who stares at him, amused and hostile.*

BROKEN ROCK: The sun is almost above the trees.
You look tired. What hungry woman kept you up so
late?

SLEEPING WATER: No woman.

BROKEN ROCK: *walking across to the top of the
earthen ramp and down to SLEEPING WATER at stage
level* Haven't we always had a share in each other's
pleasures? But no more. We share nothing. You have
other business and no time to spend with Broken Rock.

SLEEPING WATER: You must be getting ugly in your
old age. You never used to have trouble finding women
for yourself. I can remember them standing in line.

BROKEN ROCK: *laughing and putting his arm roughly around SLEEPING WATER* Ha! They still do! I have a trick. At the right moment, I whisper in their ears, "Broken Rock has fallen asleep. I am Iouskeha. I have stolen Broken Rock's body. I am strong as a bear. I am as swollen as a bull moose in heat. I am Iouskeha!" Why, their bodies tremble like leaves! Their eyes roll around in their heads! They stand in line to be mated to Iouskeha!

SLEEPING WATER: *laughing and slipping out of his grasp* My brother, you are a great liar!

BROKEN ROCK: *laughing with him, then suddenly serious* And what lies does the Blackrobe tell you? *They stare at each other in silence for a moment.* You and I were like each other's shadows, but now the Blackrobe has taken my place. When I speak to you, you make a small answer and walk away.

SLEEPING WATER: We are friends, Broken Rock, just as before.

BROKEN ROCK: No. The Blackrobe comes between us. Like a woman, he turns you against me. He fills your head full of stupidities. I am ashamed for you, because you begin to believe him.

SLEEPING WATER: *turning away* I believe nothing he says!

BROKEN ROCK: I know you. *He reaches out and taps SLEEPING WATER lightly on the side of the face.* I know this face. *He hits SLEEPING WATER with his open hand, harder.* Like a puppy, looking up at its bitch, when the Blackrobe speaks.

SLEEPING WATER: *knocking his hand away* I am tired and cold.

He turns to go.

BROKEN ROCK: Perhaps I was wrong!

SLEEPING WATER stops and turns to him.

BROKEN ROCK: Perhaps you and the Blackrobe are
lovers. Is that it? Lovers!   *He throws SLEEPING
WATER to the ground.*   Laugh, Sleeping Water, I
make a joke. He is your woman!

*He stands over SLEEPING WATER and laughs. SLEEPING
WATER gets up.*

BROKEN ROCK: Is that what all this closeness is about?
You play with each other in the snow!   *He grabs
SLEEPING WATER fiercely about the neck.*   I make
a joke! Can you not laugh? He is your woman!   *He
hurls SLEEPING WATER from him and crouches in a
fighting position ready for SLEEPING WATER's attack.*
What is it? Before this Blackrobe, you would have leaped
at my throat like a wolf. Now you cannot laugh. You
cannot fight. You cannot even look into my eyes.

SLEEPING WATER: *getting up and speaking softly*
There are different strengths, Broken Rock. Your kind
and another. You will find this out.

BROKEN ROCK: Will I? Oh yes, my brother, we are
apart. Go in by the fire where it is warm.

*SLEEPING WATER walks to the opening under the palisade,
stage left.*

BROKEN ROCK: Sleeping Water! Sit with the women.

*SLEEPING WATER exits. BROKEN ROCK looks after him
for a moment with an expression of dismay and helpless
anger.*

BROKEN ROCK: Blackrobe . . . it is like fighting the
air. Blackrobe . . . if only I was free . . . to kill you!

Scene Six

*BROKEN ROCK rushes off, stage right. The lights go down
and out. After a pause, the lights come up slowly to a bright
warm sunlight. BLACKROBE enters from under the palisade,
stage left, his cloth blanket worn and shredded, wrapped
about his shoulders, dirty rags bound to his feet. He shuffles
a little way downstage, lost in thought, and then stops.
He looks up at the sun, feels its heat. Smiling, he puts his
hands out to capture the warmth and then brings them to
his face, as if he would wash himself in the warmth. He
hurries downstage and, sitting down, unties the rags about
his feet. He looks up as SLEEPING WATER enters at the
top of the left aisle and walks down towards him at stage
level.*

BLACKROBE: *calling*   Sleeping Water ! The sun feels
   so good! Tell me winter is over!

*SLEEPING WATER smiles and leaps to the stage, with
a joyful cry.*

BLACKROBE: *his arms outstretched*   Winter is over!

SLEEPING WATER: Time to plant!

BLACKROBE: Winter is over!

SLEEPING WATER: Time to fish!

BLACKROBE: *laughing*   Winter is over!

SLEEPING WATER: Time to hunt! Time to trade!
   Time for the French to make us all rich again! Hia!

*SLEEPING WATER begins to dance. Immediately, the
Huron Chorus comes up — voices, drums, rattles — at a very
fast tempo which builds as SLEEPING WATER whirls around
stomping his feet in a wild dance. BLACKROBE looks at
SLEEPING WATER and around at the audience with delight.*

Awkwardly, half imitating SLEEPING WATER, half doing his own dance, he spins around joyfully, his blanket held high over his head, his cassock billowing out above his bare legs.

High up on the palisades, stage left, an old Jesuit priest, followed by two young priests, march briskly across the board ramp to the top of the earthen ramp, centrestage. They are all dressed like BLACKROBE, except that they wear their black, wide-brimmed hats and carry burlap satchels over their shoulders. SLEEPING WATER and BLACKROBE continue to dance below them, unaware of their presence. FATHER SUPERIOR turns briskly at the top of the ramp to descend downstage and see what's going on below him. He proceeds half-way down the ramp and stops and stares. The two Jesuits, equally as surprised as FATHER SUPERIOR, stand above him. The music builds.

SLEEPING WATER, in mid-dance, whirls and sees the Jesuits. A thunderous "Ha!" is heard and the music and SLEEPING WATER stop. BLACKROBE, not seeing the Jesuits, continues to spin about, tossing his blanket high into the air, then he looks at SLEEPING WATER and sees that he is staring at something upstage. BLACKROBE turns, sees FATHER SUPERIOR, and freezes. There is a moment of silence.

BLACKROBE: *unbelieving*   Father! Father Superior! Dear Father!   *He goes up the ramp and takes FATHER SUPERIOR's hand.*   How can it be you?

FATHER SUPERIOR: It is no other. Just me.

BLACKROBE: I am so glad to see you!

FATHER SUPERIOR walks downstage to look at SLEEPING WATER. BLACKROBE turns to FATHER HENRI and grasps his hand.

BLACKROBE: And you, Father Henri! How lonely it
has been! And . . .   *He looks up at the other Jesuit
who has stayed farther back. He is amazed and delighted.*
Daniel? Father Daniel!   *He rushes to him and embraces
him.*   How can you be here? It can't be!

FATHER DANIEL: *laughing*   But it is! I have followed
you, Father. Same village, same school, and now, the
same mission! Isn't it a miracle? We have talked of
nothing but Father Réjean ever since you left. And now
I have come too, my heart full of fervour to begin my
work in the new world!

BLACKROBE: Oh, Daniel! I can't believe that you're
here! But . . . it is nothing like what we imagined! It is
beyond. . . .

BROKEN ROCK enters, high up the right audience aisle.

BROKEN ROCK: *shouting in dismay*   Ravens! A flock
of Ravens!   *He rushes down to level stage centre.*
How did you come here?

FATHER SUPERIOR: We came by a trading party.

BROKEN ROCK: Not from this village! Not from this
clan!

FATHER SUPERIOR: No. From the Bear clan.

BROKEN ROCK: Then stay with them! We have little
enough room for this one!

He indicates BLACKROBE.

FATHER SUPERIOR: Oh no. We will stay here. Unless,
of course, your people do not want the gifts we've
brought?   *He moves towards the audience, addressing
them.*   Unless, of course, you do not want to trade
with the French anymore?

BROKEN ROCK: *enraged* I want nothing more to do with the French! *He turns to the audience.* Look! They send us these cackling ravens along with their kettles and knives. The price of this trade is too high!

SLEEPING WATER: Broken Rock! We have need of these things.

BROKEN ROCK: *turning to him* No, we do not! Did we have need of these things before the French came? Why can we not live without these things now?

SLEEPING WATER: This trade has done us no harm. Why should we give it up?

BROKEN ROCK: *indicating the Jesuits* Because of these ones!

SLEEPING WATER: *to FATHER SUPERIOR* Broken Rock does not speak for the rest of us. You are welcome in our land, as this Blackrobe has been before you. You will bring us good luck and good trade. You are welcome. All are friends.

He exits quickly under the palisade, stage right.

BROKEN ROCK: *following SLEEPING WATER a step, and screaming after him* We must send these Ravens back!

SLEEPING WATER disappears. BROKEN ROCK looks back at the Jesuits with an expression of dismay and helplessness. Suddenly, he spits on the ground at FATHER SUPERIOR's feet, turns and exits, stage right.

FATHER SUPERIOR: *taking a long look at the departing BROKEN ROCK before turning back to BLACKROBE* And how goes it with you, Father? You must tell us everything.

BLACKROBE: *coming down the ramp to FATHER SUPERIOR* Just to see you! To hear your voices! What joy after all these days in this bitter wilderness! I have been so alone!

FATHER HENRI: Father, what progress have you made?

BLACKROBE: I think a little progress. It is very difficult to tell. Many are listening to me now. Before, they would only laugh.

FATHER SUPERIOR: Where are the Christian Hurons? Do they live apart from the rest?

BLACKROBE: Some seek me out. They ask me questions. I am busy day and night!

FATHER DANIEL: What do your Christians number, Father? Twenty-five?

BLACKROBE: *embarrassed* No, Daniel.

FATHER DANIEL: Fifty?

BLACKROBE: No.

FATHER DANIEL: A hundred? A thousand?

BLACKROBE: Daniel! *He turns away.* Not one.

FATHER DANIEL AND FATHER HENRI: *surprised and shocked* Not one?

FATHER SUPERIOR: I understand you to say that there is not one convert in all of the Huron nation?

BLACKROBE: Oh, I could present you with a multitude of baptized heathens, if I cared nothing for our Sacred Mysteries. But what would be the good of that? They would be no more Christian than a bird or a fish. If these people were empty of all things, only waiting for us to fill them up with the sublime Spirit, then our work would be done in a day. But they are not. They are devious. They are strong and clever. And I must tell you, Father, they are firmly held by any number of dark and loathsome superstitions. They are bound by Satan himself!

FATHER SUPERIOR: You know I wouldn't have you sprinkle the baptismal water about like rain. But at the same time, we must show some progress. It is for the greater glory of God, I speak, of course. But also, there are mundane considerations.

FATHER HENRI: You understand . . . there are always these considerations.

BLACKROBE: *puzzled*   Yes . . . of course.

FATHER SUPERIOR: Even in this wilderness, we are watched most anxiously, Father. Nothing but good wishes from both the highest secular offices and from the Holy See. But we must begin to show the fruits of our labours or this support will quickly fade away.

BLACKROBE: There is one! His name is Sleeping Water.

FATHER SUPERIOR: A Christian?

BLACKROBE: No, not yet, but we are friends.

FATHER SUPERIOR: *impatiently*   Friends? Oh well, we will talk about him later. Right now, I propose we discuss our living arrangements. These crude structures the savages live in. Do you suppose they could be persuaded to build one for us?

BLACKROBE hesitates.

FATHER HENRI: We have a quantity of coloured beads, rings and small pocket knives.

BLACKROBE: Would it not be simpler to live with them, as I have done?

FATHER SUPERIOR: As you have done? How have you done, Father? I expected to find you surrounded by docile savages, newly saved, speaking to them from the text of Our Lord. Instead, I find you in the midst of some heathen celebration. Oh no, it is evident that living with the savages presents some grave risks.

FATHER HENRI: I know the nature of savages, having dealt with the Montagnais at Kebec. Their child-like curiosity will give us little privacy, even in a separate residence.

FATHER DANIEL: *gently*   Father, it is our plan to build a small chapel within the structure where we may worship in dignity and peace.

BLACKROBE: Oh, I see.

FATHER SUPERIOR: When we have consolidated ourselves, that will be the time to venture off among the neighbouring villages. But for now, we must grow strong here. Within the summer, our Superiors in France, even Father General in Rome, will receive our report of converts newly made.

BLACKROBE: How confident you all are! How . . . slight I seem. How useless!

FATHER SUPERIOR: *holding up his hand*   No! No! I don't want to hear talk like that! We shall concentrate on a glorious future in doing God's work here, and to the north and west and south, yes, across the breadth and to the very ends of this land! We have no time for failure.

BLACKROBE: Father?

FATHER SUPERIOR: *a little impatient*   What is it?

BLACKROBE: *going to his knees*   I would confess
    my sins!

*Suddenly, a sound is heard, like a massive body of people
breathing out harshly, and then in, in and out . . . building
a little as the lights start to go down.*

FATHER SUPERIOR: *looking around, alarmed*   What
    is that?

FATHER DANIEL: *frightened, moving towards BLACK-
    ROBE*   Father?

FATHER HENRI: *looking over the top of the ramp
    towards upstage*   Oh my God!

*FATHER SUPERIOR and FATHER DANIEL rush to see.
BLACKROBE remains frozen downstage, kneeling.*

FATHER SUPERIOR: Unspeakable! Savage beyond
    words! A prisoner. An Iroquois prisoner!

FATHER HENRI: They're cutting strips of flesh off
    his legs!

FATHER SUPERIOR: *in a whisper*   Oh Jesus, have
    pity on him.

FATHER DANIEL: They're cutting off his fingers!

FATHER SUPERIOR: Jesus, have pity on him.

The breathing builds orgiastically.

FATHER HENRI: They're stripping the flesh off his face!

FATHER DANIEL: They're drinking his blood!

FATHER HENRI: They're cutting out his heart!

FATHER SUPERIOR: God in heaven, be merciful!

47

There is a great cry from the Hurons and then silence. After a pause, FATHER SUPERIOR and the Jesuits back up a little, opening a path, as BROKEN ROCK appears upstage, on the top of the ramp. He walks slowly towards them, smeared in blood, holding a human heart in one hand and a long bloody knife in the other hand. He walks slowly past the Jesuits, down towards BLACKROBE, who backs up as BROKEN ROCK advances on him to stage level.

BROKEN ROCK: *coming up to BLACKROBE*
    Raven . . . this is . . . yours!

BROKEN ROCK puts the heart in BLACKROBE's hands and then backs away from him, exiting stage left. BLACKROBE stares at the heart and begins to shake, looking as if he were going to fall down.

The MARTYR creeps out of the pit and begins to laugh as the lights go down. As he laughs hysterically, harder and harder, BLACKROBE, shaking, still staring at the heart in his hands, opens his mouth wide. The MARTYR's laughter changes into one long scream.

The lights go to black and, immediately, the MARTYR's scream is cut at full volume.

ACT TWO
Scene Seven

*The lights come up to full. After a pause, FATHER
SUPERIOR enters from stage left.*

FATHER SUPERIOR: *dictating a letter*   And address
    to The Very Reverend Father Mutius Vitelleschi, General
    of the Society of Jesus, Rome.

*FATHER HENRI enters stage left, following FATHER
SUPERIOR, writing the address on the outside parchment
of the letter with a quill pen. He wears a little writing table
strapped about his neck.*

FATHER SUPERIOR: Have you got that down?

FATHER HENRI: *scribbling hurriedly*   Yes.

FATHER SUPERIOR: Say it back to me.

FATHER HENRI: The whole thing?

FATHER SUPERIOR: *a little annoyed*   Well, just the
    last part. If it's not too much trouble, Father.

FATHER HENRI: *reading* "We have had five missions in this region of the Hurons over the past year, preaching the gospel to more than ten thousand barbarians. We had the tongue, and they themselves the ears . . . and yet while they are sound in body, they do not hear. It therefore pleased God to pull their ears through a certain kind of pestilence, which is spreading over the whole country, and sending many to the grave."

FATHER SUPERIOR: I think that's well expressed. Don't you?

FATHER HENRI: Yes, Father.

FATHER SUPERIOR: And it plumbs to the very heart of the problem. There is ever the divine hand of God in the affairs of men, if one would only look for it.

FATHER HENRI: The Hurons are saying that wherever we preach, that is where the sickness is greatest.

FATHER SUPERIOR: And does that very fact not confirm my interpretation? Of course it does, and besides, we are not here to try to peer into the secret but always adorable judgments of God. We are here to convert and baptize. To make a Holy Nation out of a multitude of heathens. *He takes the letter from FATHER HENRI.* And so we shall. *He turns and walks towards offstage right.* That is quite enough work for us.

FATHER DANIEL, carrying a large mantle clock with some effort, enters down the left audience aisle, followed by SLEEPING WATER.

FATHER DANIEL: He was with us in France, Sleeping Water, and I've carried him all the way from Kebec. Eight hundred miles. Thirty-five portages.

FATHER HENRI: But he doesn't mind. He thinks of it as a special honour, don't you Father?

FATHER DANIEL: *with less enthusiasm*   Yes, Father.

FATHER HENRI: A holy burden!

SLEEPING WATER: Why does he make that noise?

FATHER HENRI: He's getting ready to tell us something. Put him down here, Father. Gently. Gently.   *He whispers to FATHER DANIEL as he puts the clock down.*   You did set it, didn't you?

FATHER DANIEL: *also whispering*   A minute from now. But I have misgivings, Father.

BLACKROBE enters from under the stage right palisade. He is holding a small Bible. He sits down on the log supports by the ramp and begins to read.

FATHER HENRI: You always have misgivings, Father. *He turns to SLEEPING WATER, who has crouched down by the clock, touching it gingerly.*   Sleeping Water, this is our Chief of the Day. He's a very powerful chief. We must always obey him, no matter where we are, no matter what we are doing. He tells us when to pray, when to work, when to get up and when to go to sleep. Now listen closely.   *He speaks to the clock.*   Are you ready, Chief? Speak!

Nothing happens. FATHER HENRI looks at FATHER DANIEL, who shrugs. Suddenly, the clock chimes four times. SLEEPING WATER stands up, delighted.

SLEEPING WATER: *laughing*   What miracle is this? It has a voice. It has a brain. Blackrobe, did you hear?

BLACKROBE: *without enthusiasm*   Yes. I heard. A miracle.

SLEEPING WATER: *to FATHER HENRI*   Have him speak again!

FATHER HENRI: No, I have something else, equally
as miraculous.   *He touches SLEEPING WATER on
the arm.*   Come a little distance with me.   *He and
SLEEPING WATER walk downstage right.*   I will
show you how clever our God allows us to be. I will
send a message from me to Father Daniel and no words
will pass my lips. Now then . . .   *He pulls out a piece
of parchment and takes the quill pen from his writing
table.*   . . . what message shall we send?

SLEEPING WATER: You say it.

FATHER HENRI: Oh no, my friend, whisper a message
in my ear. Anything at all.

SLEEPING WATER: Broken Rock calls you Ravens.
Ravens make a great noise.

FATHER HENRI: *taken back a little*   Oh . . . excellent!
He mumbles as he writes.   . . . make a great noise. All
right.   *He blows on the parchment and folds it.*
Give this to Father Daniel.   *He hands the parchment
to SLEEPING WATER.*   I will not say a word. Come
on!   *They walk upstage.*   Dear Father, Sleeping
Water has a message for you.

*SLEEPING WATER hands the message to FATHER
DANIEL.*

FATHER HENRI: Would you please tell our friend what
the message is, exactly as he spoke it to me.

He looks about, very pleased with himself.

FATHER DANIEL: *opening up the parchment*   "Broken
Rock calls you Ravens. Ravens make a great noise."

SLEEPING WATER: *turning to BLACKROBE*   It is
so! The same words as I put to him, not one out of place.

BLACKROBE: *dryly*   A miracle.

FATHER HENRI: *snatching BLACKROBE's Bible and showing it to SLEEPING WATER*   And that is exactly how God speaks to us.   *He opens up the Bible.*   Each page holds a message from God, just as that parchment held a message from you. And what does God say? *He pretends to study the open page.*   He tells us to come to your land.   *He turns another page, continuing as if reading the message.*   He tells us that you must give up your belief in other gods.   *He turns another page as SLEEPING WATER starts to move away.*   He tells us that you must only worship Him, our God, the one and only God!

SLEEPING WATER: *turning to BLACKROBE*   There is no escape from you, is there?   *He turns to the other Jesuits.*   You all speak the same!

He turns upstage and runs up the ramp.

FATHER HENRI: *yelling after him*   If you continue to worship devils instead of God, your soul will be tossed into hell! You'll suffer eternal torture! God will either lift you up into paradise or He will banish you into darkness! Forever!

SLEEPING WATER, his back to the Jesuits, stops at the very top of the ramp.

FATHER DANIEL: Father Henri! He is not listening to you!

FATHER HENRI: No, he is not listening. They do not listen! These people! You bring them the living Christ, and yet they turn from Him to their heathen gods. You show them the light and yet they retreat further into shadow.   *He turns to BLACKROBE.*   Oh yes, it is true they are hospitable enough, patient enough. But they are childish, thievish, lying, deceitful, licentious, proud and lazy!

SLEEPING WATER turns downstage, having heard the tirade. FATHER HENRI exits stage left, in a rage.

FATHER DANIEL: The Hurons are not children, after all. They do not skip joyfully into our world, do they? There must be a more dignified way to preach the Word of our Saviour.

BLACKROBE: I think there must.

FATHER DANIEL: But what is it? Every way meets the same end. To have come so far for such little results! It is beyond my understanding. Father Superior says they will deserve their fate if they do not listen to us.

BLACKROBE: If Father Superior says it, it must be true.

FATHER DANIEL: Yes. We must obey Father in everything. That is the only way. Through his wisdom, I'm sure the mission will be a success. We must all work and pray doubly hard.

BLACKROBE: If only we had more clocks, we could go through the whole Huron nation.

FATHER DANIEL: Do you find the rest of us so ridiculous?   *He picks up the clock.*   If I thought that I could save even one man's soul from eternal darkness by using this clock, then I should do so. I would carry it to the ends of the world. After all, Father, what success have any of us had without it?

FATHER DANIEL exits stage left. SLEEPING WATER comes down the ramp.

SLEEPING WATER: What people are thieves and liars?

BLACKROBE turns quickly to SLEEPING WATER.

SLEEPING WATER: What people will deserve their fate?

BLACKROBE: Sleeping Water!

SLEEPING WATER: What are those ones saying?

BLACKROBE: They don't mean what they're saying.
They're angry and tired. You must forgive them, they
are your friends!

SLEEPING WATER: They curse my people! No, they
are not my friends!

BLACKROBE: They are wrong to say those things.
They are wrong! But it is because they love your people
and because they are so afraid for them, that they
become angry. They have brought Almighty God to your
land, salvation and freedom! But your people are blind
and they turn away. That's why we are in despair, all of
us, because we know your fate is damnation and eternal
fire!   *He notices that SLEEPING WATER has turned
away.*   Sleeping Water?

SLEEPING WATER: I have chanted and called out to
my gods for many days. They do not answer me. I have
looked for a sign to prove what you say is wrong. I have
found nothing.   *He turns to BLACKROBE.*   You
talk to your God. He answers you. You go off alone
where no one can see you and you suffer for Him. You
would not do this if your God were not strong. I know
this and I am afraid! My gods do not come to me! I
would not lose my soul! What you tell me . . . It is true!
He takes off the amulets about his neck.   I trust you!
He gives the amulets to BLACKROBE.   I believe you!

BLACKROBE: Oh, Sleeping Water! I would not mislead
you!

*SLEEPING WATER grabs the amulets from BLACKROBE
and, with a cry, hurls them as hard as he can against the
ground. He stands frozen, looking down at the amulets,
expecting to be seized by demons at any moment. He*

*crouches down, looking terrified and forlorn. BLACKROBE
kneels beside him, putting his arm around him.*

SLEEPING WATER: It is done. I am . . . free . . . aren't
  I? Why do you weep? Why are you not glad?

BLACKROBE: I am glad! I am!

*FATHER SUPERIOR appears at the top of the earthen
ramp, extreme upstage, carrying a white stole.*

FATHER SUPERIOR: Sleeping Water! I am delighted!
  *He comes down to SLEEPING WATER and BLACK-
  ROBE.*   Our very first little lamb! Now don't be
  afraid. We will look after you from now on.

*He kisses the stole and puts it on, crosses himself quickly,
then trickles water from a phial in the form of a cross
on SLEEPING WATER's forehead.*

FATHER SUPERIOR: I baptize thee in the name of the
  Father and of the Son and of the Holy Ghost. Amen.

FATHER SUPERIOR and BLACKROBE cross themselves.

FATHER SUPERIOR: Stand up now, Sleeping Water.
  Stand up into a whole new world of light.

BLACKROBE: But Father . . . our Mysteries?

FATHER SUPERIOR: *brushing him off*   Yes, yes, we
  shall instruct him in our Sacred Mysteries as we go along.
  Come now, Sleeping Water, you have much to learn!
  *He helps SLEEPING WATER to his feet, and with a
  firm grip on his arm, they move away up the earthen
  ramp.*   I want you to be an example to all your people.
  This is most important. A Christian Huron, at last!

*SLEEPING WATER stops at the top of the ramp and turns
to BLACKROBE.*

SLEEPING WATER: I believe you! I would not lose my soul!

FATHER SUPERIOR: Come along now! Come along!

SLEEPING WATER and FATHER SUPERIOR exit across the palisade, stage left. BLACKROBE watches them for a moment. The lights go down.

Scene Eight

MARTYR: *singing from the pit*   Hallelujah!   *He crawls out of the pit.*   Hallelujah! Praise the Lord! *He pauses and looks at BLACKROBE.*   Why do you look that way?

BLACKROBE: I don't know!

He moves downstage right, his back to the MARTYR.

FATHER HENRI enters stage left, in Mass vestments, followed by FATHER SUPERIOR. FATHER DANIEL pushes on a small altar set for Mass, with two candles burning. SLEEPING WATER follows. FATHER DANIEL helps him do things properly. They all kneel before the altar and FATHER HENRI begins to go through the motions of the Mass, beginning with the Elevation of the Chalice.

MARTYR: You are doing God's work. You should be exaltant! A convert! All heaven is singing your praises! *He leaps down to stage level.*   Perhaps you are tired.

BLACKROBE: *going down on his knees to rest*   I have been in this wilderness too long!

MARTYR: *moving towards BLACKROBE*   Yes, that's it! Even Jesus grew tired.

BLACKROBE: *quietly* I don't think all heaven is singing my praises.

MARTYR: But I can hear them! Like I could hear the fire! Like I could hear my flesh! Like I could see Paradise through the flames!

BLACKROBE covers his face with his hands.

MARTYR: Don't turn away! You have only me!

BLACKROBE turns to him, watching him back towards stage right.

MARTYR: Christ is somewhere in the dark. I will be your guide, Réjean. Burning. Otherwise, you are lost. Hold on . . . to me.

He disappears offstage right.

Scene Nine

The lights come up around the altar. BLACKROBE watches where the MARTYR disappeared, then, as the sounds of the Mass come up, he turns and hastily crosses to stage left, genuflects and kneels in front of the altar. He is a little removed from the rest, downstage.

FATHER HENRI: *chanting* Per omnia saecula saeculorum.

THE OTHER JESUITS: Amen.

BROKEN ROCK enters stealthily, down the right audience aisle. He will watch from the shadows downstage right for a moment, and then stealthily, watching the Mass all the time, move up the earthen ramp and disappear over the top, at the end of the Mass.

FATHER HENRI: *joining his hands* Oremus:
Praeceptis salutaribus moniti, et divina institutione
formati, audemus dicere. *He extends his hands.*
Pater noster, qui es in caelis: Sanctificetur nomen tuum:
Adveniat regnum tuum: Fiat voluntas tua, sicut in caelo,
et in terra. Panem nostrum quotidianum da nobis hodie:
Et dimitte nobis debita nostra, sicut et nos dimittimus
debitoribus nostris. Et ne nos inducas in tentationem.

THE OTHER JESUITS: Sed libera nos a malo.

FATHER HENRI: Agnus Dei, qui tollis peccata mundi.

THE OTHER JESUITS: *beating their breasts* Miserere
nobis.

FATHER HENRI: Agnus Dei, qui tollis peccata mundi.

THE OTHER JESUITS: Miserere nobis.

FATHER HENRI: Agnus Dei, qui tollis peccata mundi.

THE OTHER JESUITS: Dona nobis pacem.

*FATHER HENRI turns the page, prays silently for a
moment, then takes Communion. He puts a small white
towel over his arm, picks up the chalice and turns towards
FATHER SUPERIOR, who rises. FATHER HENRI
indicates to SLEEPING WATER to get the Communion
paten near the altar. He blesses FATHER SUPERIOR,
who crosses himself and takes the towel and chalice.
FATHER HENRI takes the ciborium and they administer
Communion to the other Jesuit. BLACKROBE refuses
Communion with a motion of his head. SLEEPING WATER
holds the Communion paten under the others' mouths
so nothing falls to the ground. BROKEN ROCK exits.
FATHER HENRI tidies up the altar. SLEEPING WATER
and FATHER SUPERIOR kneel beside the other Jesuits
again.*

FATHER HENRI: *after a silent prayer*   Benedicat
vos omnipotens Deus.

He turns to face downstage, making the Sign of the Cross.

*Underneath the voice of FATHER HENRI, the sound of
the Huron Chorus begins to come up in a slow dirge — a
wailing.*

FATHER HENRI: Pater, et Filium, et Spiritus Sanctus.

THE OTHER JESUITS: Amen.

FATHER HENRI: Dominus vobiscum.

THE OTHER JESUITS: Et cum spiritu tuo.

*The Jesuits turn and slowly walk offstage left, FATHER
DANIEL pushing the altar. BLACKROBE and SLEEPING
WATER remain. The sound of the Huron Chorus comes
up, voices wailing in unison; drums and rattles beating.
SLEEPING WATER has taken a baptismal phial from the
altar. BLACKROBE, followed by SLEEPING WATER,
walks slowly downstage as the lights go down. They look
into the audience.*

BLACKROBE: The sickness . . . is everywhere! Is there
not one longhouse in all the Huron nation safe from this
plague?

SLEEPING WATER: The shamans say Ataenstic walks
through the land, sores, like hands, reaching out of her
body, her eyes drowning in pus. She touches everyone.

*BLACKROBE steps up onto the elevated stage and speaks
despairingly to the audience.*

BLACKROBE: Here I am. Once again. God's light.
*He turns and wets his fingers in the phial SLEEPING
WATER holds, standing below him, then turns back
to the audience.*   I baptize thee in the name of the

Father and of the Son and of the Holy Ghost. Oh, Sleeping Water, the old people are dying! *He dips his fingers in the phial again.* I baptize thee in the name of the Father and of the Son and of the Holy Ghost. Oh, Sleeping Water, the children are dying! *He dips his fingers again.* I baptize thee in the name of the Father and of the Son and of the Holy Ghost. *He cries out.* God . . . will it not stop?

Immediately, the Huron Chorus is silent. The lights come up on BROKEN ROCK, who is standing on the earthen ramp. He looks haggard and tired. He holds a thick gnarled stick in his hand.

BROKEN ROCK: It is not Ataenstic who walks through our land. It is you.

He moves downstage towards BLACKROBE and SLEEPING WATER. BLACKROBE comes back down to stage level.

BROKEN ROCK: You open your Raven's mouth and death flies out. Our flesh is corrupted by your demons. *He indicates SLEEPING WATER.* You tame this Huron like a dog. The ones you cannot tame, you kill! Keep away from us, Raven. Do not come near anymore. Your dog . . . your dog . . . destroys my mind!

He lashes out viciously at SLEEPING WATER with the stick, catching him on the side of the head. SLEEPING WATER crumbles to the ground. BROKEN ROCK raises his hand for a second blow.

BLACKROBE: *crying out* Do not strike him again! *He bends down to SLEEPING WATER.* Oh, my brother!

BROKEN ROCK seizes BLACKROBE, pulling him away from SLEEPING WATER. He puts his hand under BLACKROBE's chin and pushes up cruelly, forcing BLACKROBE's head back.

BROKEN ROCK: He is not your brother! Is he? Is he?

BROKEN ROCK, his eyes wide, continues to push BLACKROBE. BLACKROBE sucks in air and pulls weakly against BROKEN ROCK's arm.

BROKEN ROCK: Say he is not your brother! Say he is mine! *With a little more pressure, he could break BLACKROBE's neck, but suddenly, he lets him go.* Go! Run! Before I go against the councils! Before I kill you!

BLACKROBE scrambles away from him, upstage, crawling part of the way up the earthen ramp. BROKEN ROCK turns back to SLEEPING WATER, who is lying senseless on the ground.

BROKEN ROCK: *in anguish* Look! Look at this Huron dog!

BROKEN ROCK kneels beside SLEEPING WATER, touching his hand to SLEEPING WATER's head. There is blood. He holds SLEEPING WATER to him. They are isolated in a pool of light.

BLACKROBE: Oh, darkness all about in this awesome land! Oh, rock hard beneath the daylight shimmerings of water and grasses and trees! And where is God?

MARTYR: *his arms spread wide, marching over the top of the ramp above BLACKROBE* Réjean . . . Réjean . . . He is with you! Can't you see the wondrous miracles you have wrought? All is harmony and good will, a nation of heathens lifted unto grace! It is all your doing, with God on your right shoulder and Jesus on your left. You are a worker of miracles!

BLACKROBE: But there is ruin all about me! It was not so before I came. They were strong!

MARTYR: They were heathens, Réjean, and now the grace of God shines all about!

BLACKROBE: Oh, but their children rot in their arms!

MARTYR: No! No! That is a lie!

BLACKROBE: Oh, but they are dying!

MARTYR: No! No! They don't die! All is light! All is peace! We must sing, Réjean. Sing!

The MARTYR and BLACKROBE sing together: the MARTYR, vibrant; BLACKROBE, faltering. They march up the ramp, the MARTYR leading, and disappear upstage.

MARTYR AND BLACKROBE: Lo, God is here, let us adore . . . and own how dreadful is this place. Let all . . . within us . . . feel His power . . . and silent . . . bow . . . before His face. . . .

The lights go down and out.

Scene Ten

After a moment, FATHER HENRI and FATHER DANIEL enter in the darkness, on the palisades, to the left and right, carrying candles and singing plain chant. When they reach the top of the ramp, they turn and walk down it, abreast, passing a man standing halfway down the ramp. The lights come up a little. It is BROKEN ROCK standing beside the ramp, motionless, facing upstage. The Jesuits ignore him.

FATHER HENRI AND FATHER DANIEL: *chanting together*   Spiritus Domini, replevit arbear terrarum, alleluia . . .

They proceed offstage right of stage level, continuing their plain chant. The lights come up and FATHER SUPERIOR walks on briskly from stage left, carrying a large scroll under his arm.

FATHER SUPERIOR: Ah, Broken Rock, there you are. You wanted to see me?

BROKEN ROCK turns and stares stonily at him.

FATHER SUPERIOR: Well, what is it? Don't tell me that you, of all people, have suddenly seen the light?

BROKEN ROCK: *coming slowly down the ramp to stage level*   This Jesus that you have brought in secret into our land. This corpse. I have seen you eat its flesh. I have seen you drink its blood. You have hidden it from our eyes and you feed on it. It makes you grow strong, but it sickens my people and we die!

FATHER SUPERIOR: *laughing and shaking his head* Really, Broken Rock! Your grasp of the Eucharist is less than perfect. You should come for instruction. Do you know that our mission flourishes? We have baptized over a thousand! And now we have a multitude of Frenchmen here at our service. It is time for a bolder plan!

BROKEN ROCK: You do not need this corpse any longer. You are strong enough. If you would show it to me, I could burn it and my people would get well again.

FATHER SUPERIOR: Oh no, we are not strong enough yet. We are expanding our village. We are building with stone. You will be amazed!

BROKEN ROCK: I am amazed already. My people die like fish thrown out upon the shore.   *He walks downstage away from FATHER SUPERIOR.*   The

Iroquois know now how weak we are. Already they move towards our land. We have called councils, but our fathers cannot make up their minds about you. Some say to send you back to Kebec. Others say we must trade for guns. *He turns to FATHER SUPERIOR.* I stand up in council and I say — you should die if you do not show us this corpse!

FATHER SUPERIOR: Save your breath, Broken Rock. We won't be going back to Kebec and we won't be sport for you at the torture post. You have seen our soldiers, haven't you? Better that you should come for instruction. Better that you prepare your soul to meet Almighty God. You'll have much to answer for, I'm sure.

BROKEN ROCK: Our fathers talk in council, but as they talk, they die. They talk in circles and they die!

FATHER SUPERIOR: Then they should have listened to us, shouldn't they? You need only to look around you . . . at your people . . . and at us in perfect health . . . to see what you should have done. We have been here all along, but we will wait a little while longer. We have time.

He turns to exit, stage left.

BROKEN ROCK: *calling after him* You Ravens eat the dead! You open up your mouths to us and we are consumed by sickness. You must show me this corpse!

FATHER SUPERIOR: *turning back to him* Broken Rock . . . I must show you . . . nothing!

He exits, stage left.

The lights go down. BROKEN ROCK backs up a step. Suddenly, a rattle sound, amplified and menacing, is heard. BROKEN ROCK turns and looks around.

BROKEN ROCK: Do I have to rip up the earth with my hands?

The rattle sounds again, like a hiss. BROKEN ROCK moves towards downstage right.

BROKEN ROCK: Do I have to tear out the trees and push aside the rocks? Do I have to crawl like a snake through the underbrush?   *He screams out the words.*   Can I smell it out when our whole land stinks of death? Where is it?   *He is now frantic.*   Somewhere! Hidden! Somewhere! In the dark! Somewhere!

SLEEPING WATER enters, stage right.

SLEEPING WATER: Broken Rock! Stop! You cannot find what you're looking for.

BROKEN ROCK: I will find it! I will destroy it!

SLEEPING WATER: You don't understand. Jesus is everywhere. Jesus is the very light.

BROKEN ROCK: *advancing on him*   You would put flaming coals in my eyes. You would cut long strips of flesh from my legs. You would boil my brains and eat them!

SLEEPING WATER: I would not!

BROKEN ROCK: Then why do you mouth these Raven words? Don't talk to me of this Jesus! Show me where they hide his stinking corpse!

SLEEPING WATER: There is no corpse! It is bread that the Blackrobes eat. It is a thing called wine that they drink. But when they put it in their mouths, the bread turns to the Flesh of Jesus and the wine turns to His Blood. It is magic.

BROKEN ROCK: *turning away* The flesh of my people, the blood of my people, these are not magic things. They are real . . . and they wither away! Our shamans crawl through the dust from village to village. They can't even cure themselves. They lie in the dust like starving dogs. They die. *He is overcome with emotion.* Our chiefs and captains are all dead!

SLEEPING WATER: I know this.

BROKEN ROCK: A nation of thirty thousand! Twenty thousand of these are dead!

SLEEPING WATER: These are my people too!

BROKEN WATER: *turning on him* No! You have no people. You have left them to seek out the Blackrobe's God. You are very lucky. The air is full of Him! *He walks up the ramp. He looks exhausted. At the top of the ramp he turns to SLEEPING WATER.* You . . . go back to the Blackrobes. They have food. They are well and happy. This is their land now.

He exits across the palisade, stage right.

Scene Eleven

SLEEPING WATER stands motionless for a long moment, looking after BROKEN ROCK. The lights change. He is now in SAINTE-MARIE. The sound of construction and hammers and saws is heard. SLEEPING WATER turns slowly, looking about him with curiosity and awe.

FATHER SUPERIOR: *entering briskly from stage left, carrying building plans for Sainte-Marie* Sleeping Water! We were so worried about you! Father Réjean told us how you had been struck down by Broken Rock. Are you alright?

SLEEPING WATER: Yes, Father. I'm alright. I must
see Father Réjean.

FATHER SUPERIOR: Well, who knows where Father
Réjean is. He's here. He's there. Like a ghost. Are you
sure you're alright?

SLEEPING WATER: Yes, Father.

He looks around him.

FATHER SUPERIOR: Our buildings are much different
from the Huron longhouse, aren't they? Taller and
stronger. This village will stand a hundred years. It will
never have to be moved.   *He indicates areas offstage
to the left and around to upstage right.*   We are
constructing a chapel for the worship of God. Do you
understand, Sleeping Water? This is truly the house of
God in the wilderness. And here is where we sleep and
study. This is where our workmen live. Our stables,
blacksmith and carpenter shops, our cookhouse, our
granary. The purpose of these buildings is a mystery
to you now, my friend. But in time, with God's good
will, these mysteries will be revealed and you will be as
familiar with these things as I am.

SLEEPING WATER: Father, I am hungry. There is no
food in the villages.

FATHER SUPERIOR: And so you shall be fed! God
has been good to us and has blessed our fields with a
bountiful harvest.

SLEEPING WATER: Father, the people are starving.

FATHER SUPERIOR: Bring them to us, Sleeping Water.
We are the servants of your people just as we are the
servants of God. We will do what we can. Bring them
to us!

The construction sounds fade away. FATHER SUPERIOR watches as SLEEPING WATER, looking tired and unsteady, walks up the right aisle.

FATHER SUPERIOR: *to himself*   How fortune has turned about, making those who were at the mercy of the savages, providers to the whole countryside! And those that were so haughty and proud, now beggars at our door! Oh, who could doubt but there is the Hand of God in this? It is a rebuke to them for turning their backs on the light that was there and seeking out the darkest corners. The plague and the famine are nothing but the bitter fruits of God's displeasure. I see great hope in this despair!   *He shouts out in joy.*   Come in, come in to us at Sainte-Marie!

SLEEPING WATER reaches the top of the aisle and sits down wearily on a step.

FATHER SUPERIOR: *shouting offstage towards the left*   Fathers! The children are coming! Hurry! Hurry!

FATHER DANIEL and FATHER HENRI enter, stage left, carrying a large basket between them, filled with small loaves of bread. They hurry up the left audience aisle. BLACK-ROBE enters from under the palisade, stage right, and watches the Jesuits hurry up the aisle and out.

FATHER SUPERIOR: Is this not a miracle, Father? We shall have converts by the thousands!

BLACKROBE: Another miracle . . . Oh God . . . like the clock!

FATHER SUPERIOR: I beg your pardon, Father?

BLACKROBE: Forgive me. I am . . . confused by all this excitement!

FATHER SUPERIOR: *shrugging*   It is forgotten. I'm sure it doesn't need to be forgiven, dear Father.   *He looks around with enthusiasm.*   Bless God, this response to Sainte-Marie is staggering! We should seriously consider expansion.

BLACKROBE: Expansion? But Father, we have not yet completed what we have begun! Nothing is finished!

FATHER SUPERIOR: You do not necessarily have to finish one thing to begin another. You must be flexible, prepared always to take advantage of any change. You are too conservative. The mission to the savages is a work of major proportions. It demands energy and imagination. Yes, I am convinced. We shall extend the boundaries of Sainte-Marie in this direction . . .
He points offstage, to the left.   . . . to encompass a settlement of Christian Hurons. Surely we will have more than enough new Christians to fill the area three times over and it is always wise to keep the Christian living apart from the heathen, for fear the Christian forgets himself.   *He smiles at BLACKROBE.*   You, especially, must agree with that.

BLACKROBE: Yes. One does forget oneself when surrounded by heathens such as these. A mortal sin, Father.

FATHER SUPERIOR: And we must build them a church in their own quarters, separate from our chapel.

SLEEPING WATER begins to walk slowly, unsteadily, down towards BLACKROBE, who does not see him.

BLACKROBE: *walking a little way away from FATHER SUPERIOR, to stage right*   Build them a hospital too, for they have need of one.

FATHER SUPERIOR: Yes. We will construct a suitable building and our French surgeon will administer to them there.

BLACKROBE: Consecrate a plot of land for a graveyard, for they will have need of it.

FATHER SUPERIOR: *impatiently*   Yes. Yes. We will look after all these things. Our children will want for nothing! We will find them a suitable place to rest and then, if they would eat again, they must set to work on a longhouse, to be built within our compound. And I shall set to work on the plans for their church. The church of St. Joseph, we shall call it. Oh, there is so much to be done!

FATHER SUPERIOR exits, stage left. SLEEPING WATER reaches stage level and is finally noticed by BLACKROBE.

BLACKROBE: Sleeping Water! Is that you?   *He rushes to him and embraces him.*   My brother, how are you?

SLEEPING WATER: Broken Rock said I was not of my people anymore. He said I was a stranger. There was a time, oh a long time ago, when Broken Rock loved me. But now, I am something other than a Huron.   *He is pleading now.*   What am I?

BLACKROBE: You are a Christian!   *He notices that SLEEPING WATER seems about to collapse.*   What is it?

He grabs hold of SLEEPING WATER.

SLEEPING WATER: I am sick!   *He is panting heavily.* What is happening to me? You said I would be strong!

BLACKROBE: Oh no! Don't talk! I cannot bear it!

SLEEPING WATER: *clinging to BLACKROBE* When you first came into our country, I looked after you.

BLACKROBE: Yes!

SLEEPING WATER: I was your friend!

BLACKROBE: Yes!

SLEEPING WATER: You must look after me!

BLACKROBE: What would you have me do? Weep for
you? Oh, if tears could make you well again, then I
would weep tears enough to drown this land. But I am
powerless. I can do nothing!

SLEEPING WATER: *pleading with him*   Help me!

BLACKROBE: I can't!   *He breaks away from
SLEEPING WATER.*   Go with the others. They
will look after you.

SLEEPING WATER: But it was you I trusted. It was you
who said I must forsake my own gods to save my soul!

BLACKROBE: *with his back to SLEEPING WATER*
Sickness is not the end of your soul. It is the beginning.
You have proclaimed your faith in God through Jesus
Christ. If you are sincere in this, then you are safely in
the hands of God. I can do nothing more.

SLEEPING WATER: *frightened*   Don't leave me!

BLACKROBE: *quietly, resigned*   Please go in with the
others. There is a small quantity of medicine. There is
a man here skilled in sickness such as this. God be willing,
you will not die.

SLEEPING WATER: I gave you my soul!

BLACKROBE: No! Not me! You gave it to God. Not me!

SLEEPING WATER: *rising, after a pause*   I am lost
and afraid. Pray for me, Father.

He stares at BLACKROBE for a moment, and then turns and walks unsteadily to stage left and exits.

Scene Twelve

The lights go down, leaving BLACKROBE in a spotlight.

BLACKROBE: *falling to his knees*   Ohhh! What have I done? Jesus! I need you now. Tell me that all things are planned. Show me that pain is good. Tell me about Paradise! Make me forget about this world. Oh Jesus, I am tired. This cross weighs me down until my soul would break!   *He takes off his crucifix and holds it up.* Take it from me!

He drops the crucifix and bows his head slowly, his arms falling limply to his sides.

A silhouette of a man is seen at the top of the earthen ramp, upstage. Slowly, a brilliant light comes up on him. He is an IROQUOIS WARRIOR, his face and body streaked with bright war paint, his hair a thick bristling brushcut, shaved to the scalp on the sides. He wears a loincloth, moccasins and leggings, and a long knife hangs from his waist. He carries a musket and holds it against his chest. He stands motionless, staring fiercely out towards the audience. He looks left and right, half turns and disappears silently, upstage, over the ramp.

The lights go down as the sound of a raging fire comes up. The sky turns red and is flickering. BLACKROBE remains downstage, oblivious to everything, his head bowed. FATHER SUPERIOR appears high upon the palisade, stage left. He is very excited.

FATHER SUPERIOR: Father! Sainte-Marie burns!

BLACKROBE looks up at him. FATHER HENRI and FATHER DANIEL run down the audience aisles, left and right, holding burning torches.

FATHER SUPERIOR: We have put it to the torch. The Iroquois have overrun the countryside, but they will never have the pleasure of desecrating our work! *He walks along the wooden ramp to stage centre.* Oh, my raging, dying Sainte-Marie! All our labour! Destroyed! *He rushes down the earthen ramp.* This is not the end for us! We shall build new missions. We shall bring Christ to other nations. We shall keep the gates of this trade open for Mother France!

FATHER HENRI: We are far from finished here. We will not give up.

FATHER DANIEL: What would be the sense of it if we were to flee back to Kebec? What would we have accomplished?

FATHER SUPERIOR: Come along, Father. We must go before the Iroquois see the flames. The rafts are loaded and ready to set off down the river. *He rushes off towards stage right.* Hurry! Hurry! For God's sake, they'll be on us in a minute!

He exits stage right, followed by FATHER HENRI. FATHER DANIEL stops and turns back to BLACKROBE. They stare at each other for a moment, then FATHER DANIEL rushes off. BLACKROBE turns to the flames, upstage, and walks slowly towards the ramp.

BLACKROBE: Sainte-Marie!

BROKEN ROCK enters from the shadows, stage left. His voice is hoarse and weak.

BROKEN ROCK: I . . . beg . . . of . . . you.

BROKEN ROCK is now just a shell of the physical man he was before. His face is gaunt, his eyes sunken. His hair is matted and hanging in tatters about his face. He wears a ragged shirt and his leggings are torn. He stands before BLACKROBE, his head down.

BROKEN ROCK: Let me eat of it. Let me drink of it. So that I too will be strong!   *He kneels before BLACKROBE and picks up the crucifix.*   The Flesh of your God. The Blood of your God.

BLACKROBE: Oh, would you stand, Brother? Please. I cannot endure you kneeling before me!

BROKEN ROCK: I would share in the corpse of this Jesus. I would join you in your strength. I would deny my gods.

BLACKROBE: Oh, I would rather my eyes dry up and turn to dust than see you such as this! I have no strength to give.

BROKEN ROCK: But there is a magic sign for this corpse. *He crosses himself vaguely in imitation of the Jesuits.* There is much praying. There are many words of instruction. There is sprinkling of water.

BLACKROBE: Yes. All that. But none of it will do any good. I cannot make you well again.

BROKEN ROCK: But it is this corpse that brings the sickness to my people.

BLACKROBE: There is no corpse!

BROKEN ROCK: You lie! You must take me to it. If I could find it . . . if I could destroy it, my people would be renewed!   *He pulls BLACKROBE to his knees before him.*   I beg of you! Show it to me!

BLACKROBE: Broken Rock! There is no magic corpse! There is no solution! Nothing!

After a long pause, BROKEN ROCK puts the crucifix on the ground and rises to his feet.

BROKEN ROCK: Oh, Raven . . . listen to me. I go to die in honour before the Iroquois. Never again will I have to see my people lie like dogs beneath your feet.   *He backs up towards stage left.*   You will not see me again unless you come out into the wilderness, crying after death.

BROKEN ROCK exits, stage left. BLACKROBE stares after him, still on his knees. The MARTYR crawls out of the pit.

MARTYR: Ah, Réjean! Precious boy! You have done your work well! Who would have thought we'd have had such a success?

BLACKROBE: *still staring at stage left*   The world lies about me in ruins.

MARTYR: *coming down to level stage centre*   You think too much of this world! You don't think enough of the world to come.

BLACKROBE: I think only of the world to come! *He gets up and crosses to downstage centre.*   But death and I have walked through this land, arm in arm. Just count the souls I've sent to heaven! I am a saint!

He tries to laugh, but it almost sounds like a cry.

MARTYR: *circling upstage, behind BLACKROBE* And to think we have come this far! You and I! We must be close to it by now.

BLACKROBE: Jesus, forgive me! Somehow I have failed. I cannot see your love in this!

76

MARTYR: *moving up the ramp*   I hung on an axletree, burning to death. While Nero drank his wine. He didn't even bother to look at me!

BLACKROBE: *ignoring the MARTYR and picking up the crucifix*   And yet I do love You!

MARTYR: The flames started at my head.

BLACKROBE: Beyond this nightmare . . . Jesus . . . still reaching out . . .

MARTYR: And worked down to my feet.

BLACKROBE: It comes apart . . . the wilderness is all . . . and Jesus nailed against the Cross . . . again and again! O my Jesus, even in ruin and desolation, Your love cries out! O my Jesus, it is at an end. I surrender my soul to darkness . . . or to You.

BLACKROBE puts his crucifix back on and slowly, deliberately, turns and walks towards stage left.

MARTYR: Just like a candle.   *He sees that BLACK-ROBE is leaving him. He becomes unsure, his voice trails off.*   It was amusing . . . to the ladies . . . Réjean?   *He screams after BLACKROBE.*   Réjean!

Immediately, the lights go down and out. There are sounds of thunder and lightning flashes. The lights come up slowly — a blue smoky light. BROKEN ROCK sits listlessly on the ground, stage right. He mumbles a sad low chant, staring at the ground. An iron pot sits on a circle of stones and boils over a small fire beside him. The IROQUOIS LEADER, the one with the musket, stands at the top of the earthen ramp. He can only be seen momentarily in the flashes of lightning. Suddenly, he fires his musket.

The lights come up immediately. BROKEN ROCK staggers to his feet, facing upstage. The IROQUOIS LEADER, now in a blaze of light, raises his musket over his head, stares down

*at BROKEN ROCK and screams, not a war-whoop, but one
prolonged blood-chilling scream. Suddenly, three other
IROQUOIS WARRIORS with war paint, carrying metal
hatchets and loops of rawhide appear: one from stage right;
the other two running down the aisles, left and right.
BROKEN ROCK turns to face them. They close in.*

*The IROQUOIS LEADER moves quickly down the ramp
and catches BROKEN ROCK behind the head with a blow
from the butt of his musket. BROKEN ROCK falls to the
ground. One of the IROQUOIS loops a length of rawhide
around his neck and pulls him up sharply. The IROQUOIS
LEADER raises his musket to deliver another blow to
BROKEN ROCK's upturned face, just as BLACKROBE,
half running, half staggering, comes up over the ramp,
upstage, and runs down it a little way before stopping.
He stares down at the IROQUOIS. They spread out below
him, forgetting BROKEN ROCK. Slowly, BLACKROBE
puts out his arms.*

*The IROQUOIS, together, begin to scream one long piercing
note and BLACKROBE starts to walk through the sound
towards them. Two of the IROQUOIS go up the ramp a
little to him, put their hands on his shoulders and rip off
his cassock. Immediately, the screaming stops. BLACKROBE
stands naked, except for a linen loincloth. He walks in a
daze down to stage level. BROKEN ROCK picks up
the iron pot of boiling water. A piece of rawhide trails from
his neck. He holds the pot over his head and advances on
BLACKROBE.*

BROKEN ROCK: Raven . . . I baptize thee!

*BROKEN ROCK pours the boiling water over BLACKROBE's
head. BLACKROBE stiffens with pain, his mouth opens in
a soundless scream. Immediately, one of the IROQUOIS
clubs BROKEN ROCK to death, the pot falling from his
hands as he falls to the ground. At the same time, the two
IROQUOIS behind BLACKROBE, with a ringing cry, lift
him up high and, running with him, toss him onto a long
knife held out at arms length by the IROQUOIS LEADER,*

who is crouched a little downstage. The knife plunges deep into BLACKROBE's stomach. He quivers on the end of the knife for a moment, then the IROQUOIS LEADER withdraws the knife and stands back. He and one of the other IROQUOIS exit silently, stage left. The other two IROQUOIS back up and exit, stage right.

BLACKROBE remains on his feet for a moment, then sinks to his knees. Slowly, he stretches out on the ground, his hand moving towards BROKEN ROCK. His hand quivers and goes limp. He dies. The two men lie dead, a little way apart from each other, at the bottom of the ramp.

The lights go down slightly and then come up very brightly to indicate a new day. SLEEPING WATER enters over the top of the earthen ramp, upstage. He walks down the ramp slowly and passes between the bodies of BROKEN ROCK and BLACKROBE. He looks at them, then he walks a little further downstage. His voice is flat, almost devoid of expression.

SLEEPING WATER: *speaking to the audience*   The Blackrobes run before the Iroquois. Our Huron villages smoulder black and dead. What am I now, left alone? Not Huron, for they don't exist. Not Christian, for they have fled. The fever has lifted, and like a man who cannot die, captive in my broken land, I breathe, I open up my hands and eyes . . . I live!

The lights come down very slowly, leaving the stage in darkness.